Christmas Scenes

Coloring Book

Relaxing stress relief for adults and great fun for kids.

Christmas Scenes Coloring Book

Copyright CWT Publishing 2020

All rights reserved. No part of this publication may be reproduced, distributed, or transmitted in any form or by any means.

ISBN: 9798567553671

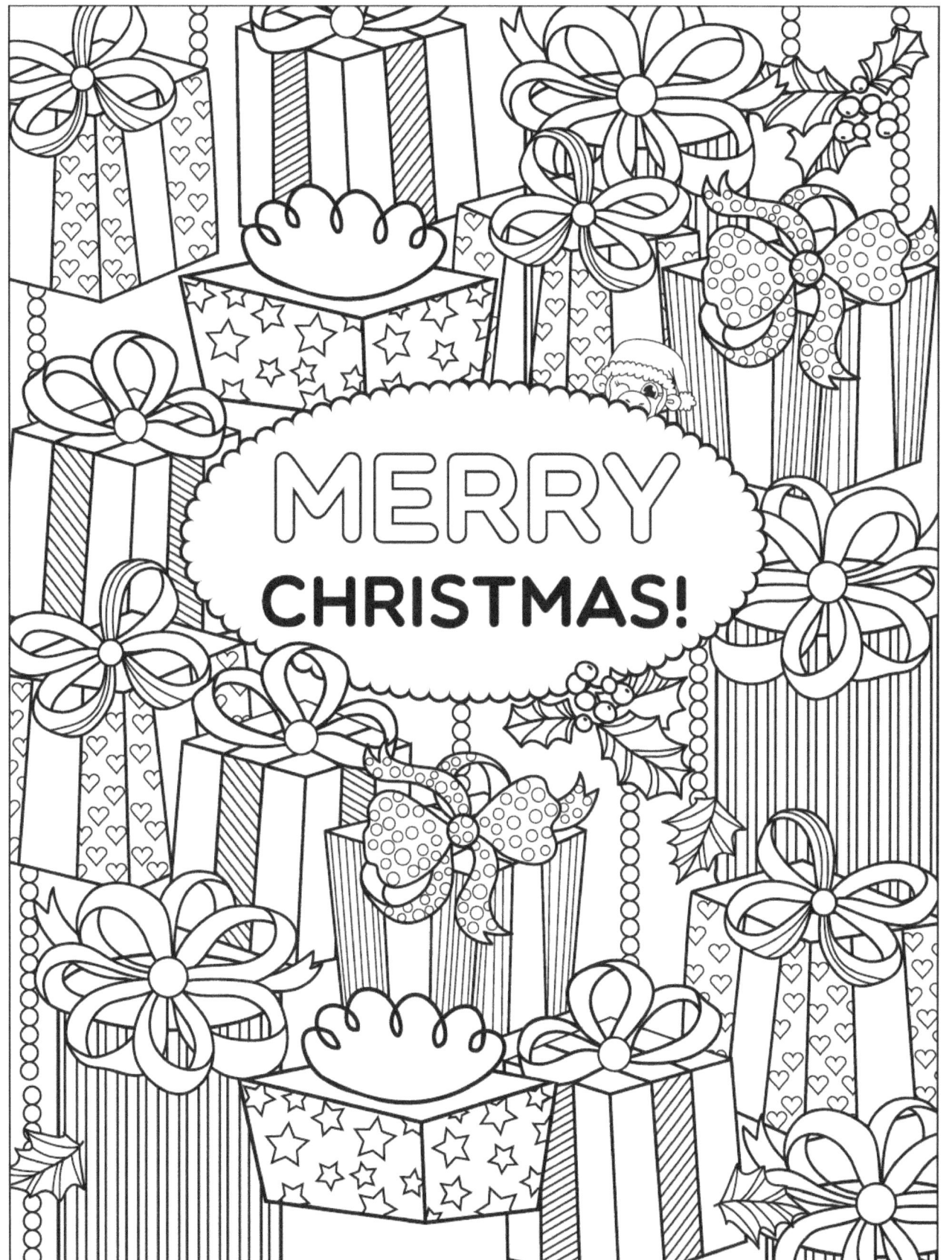

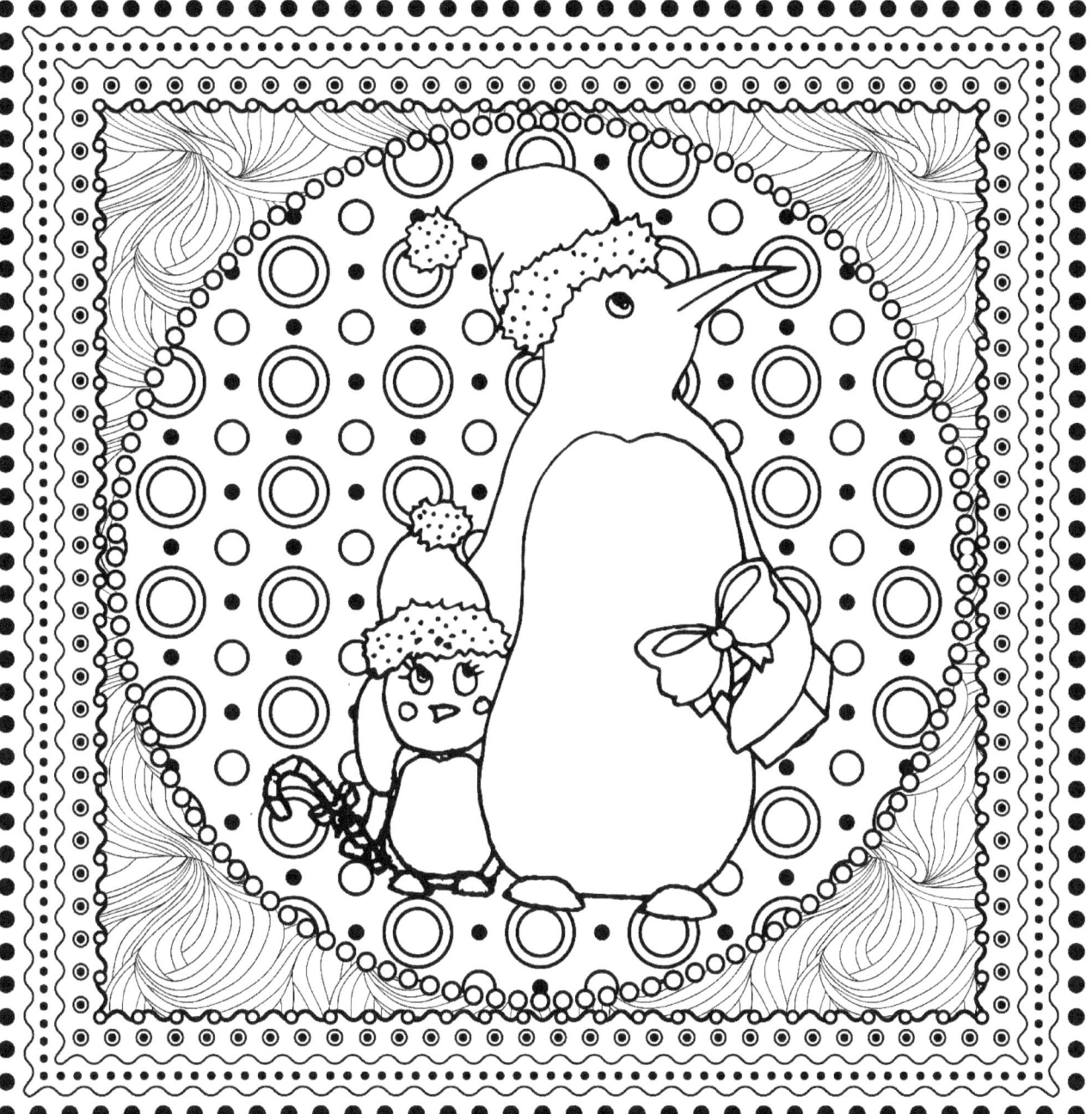

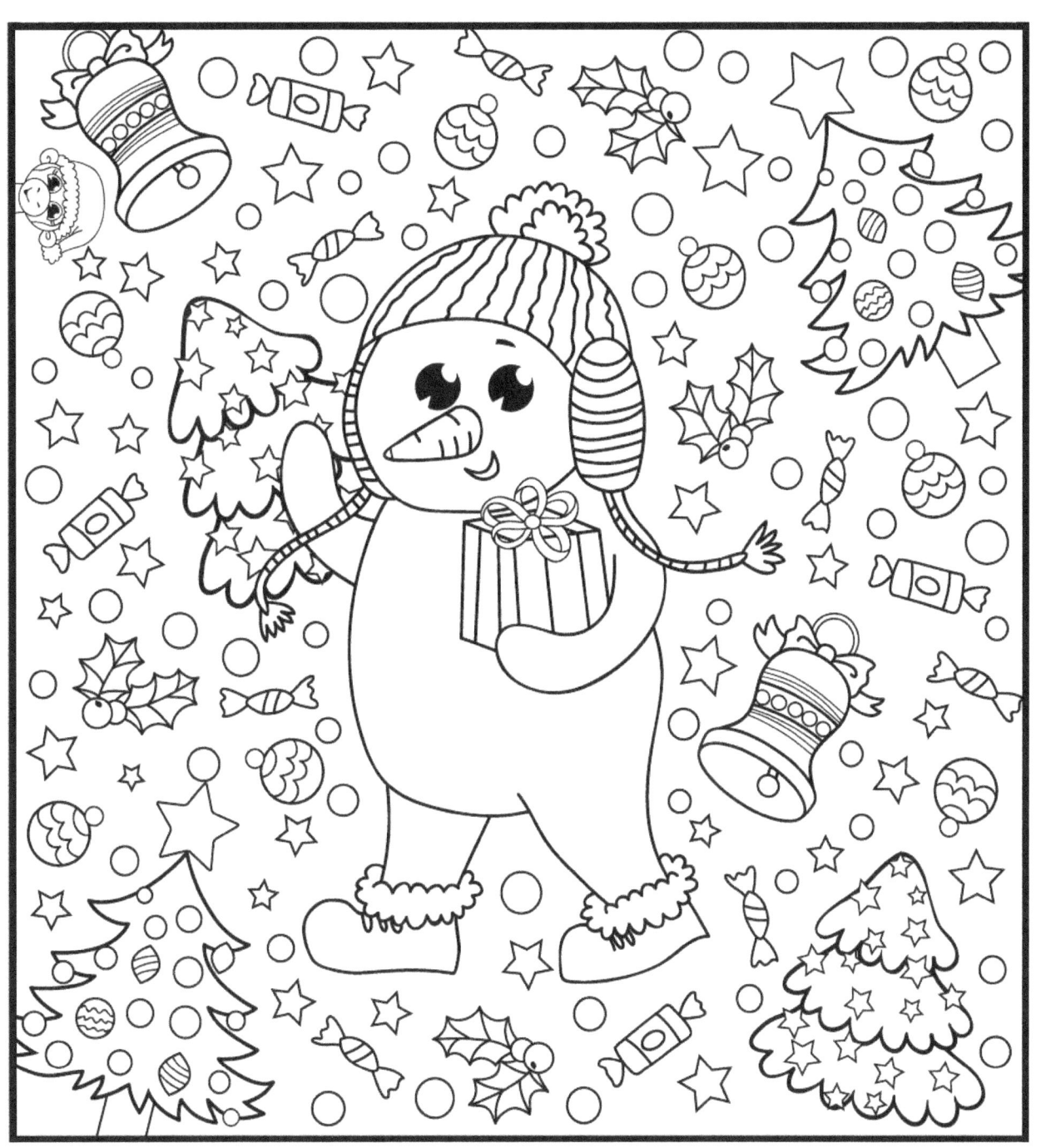

4

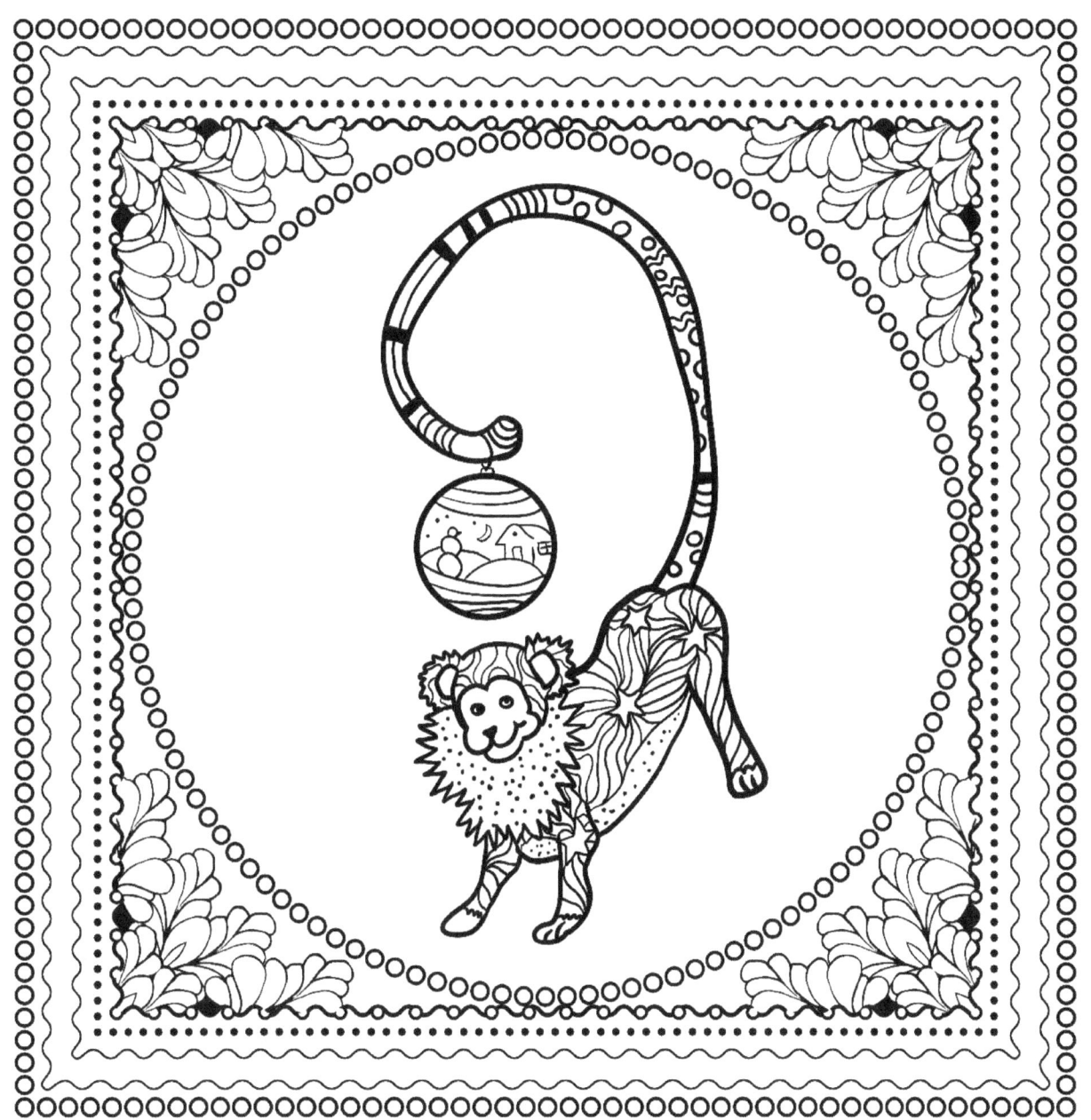

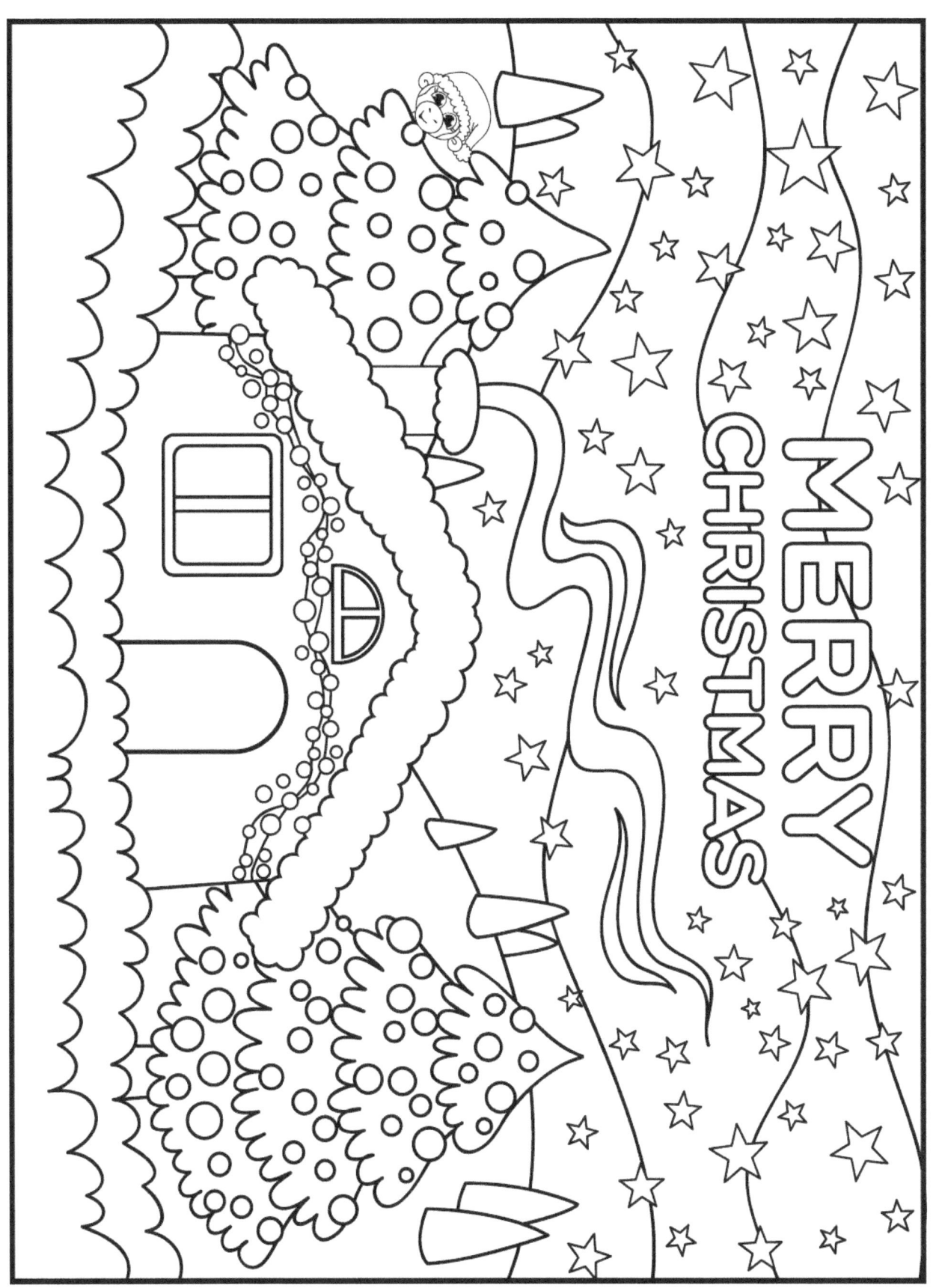

6

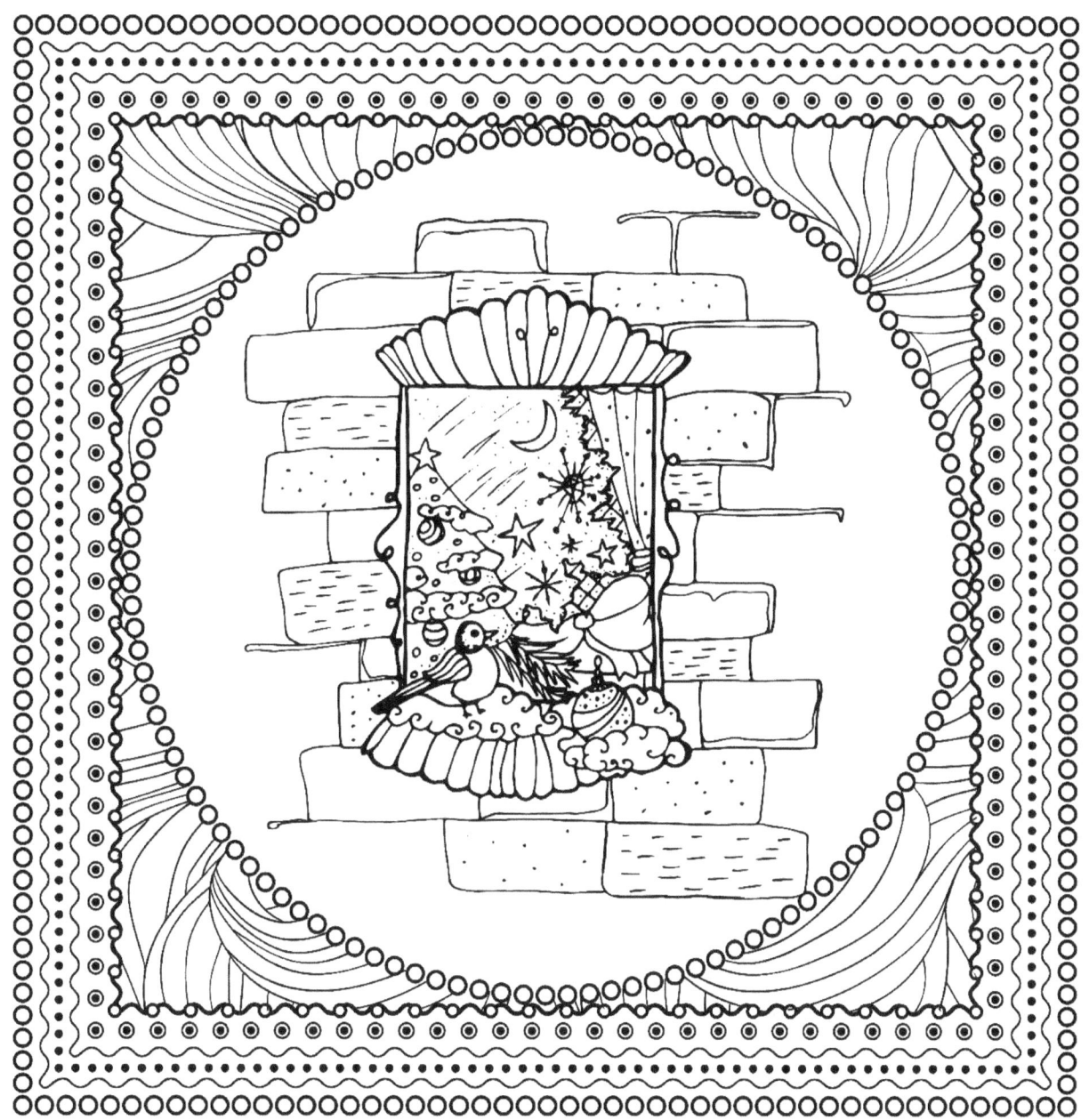

7

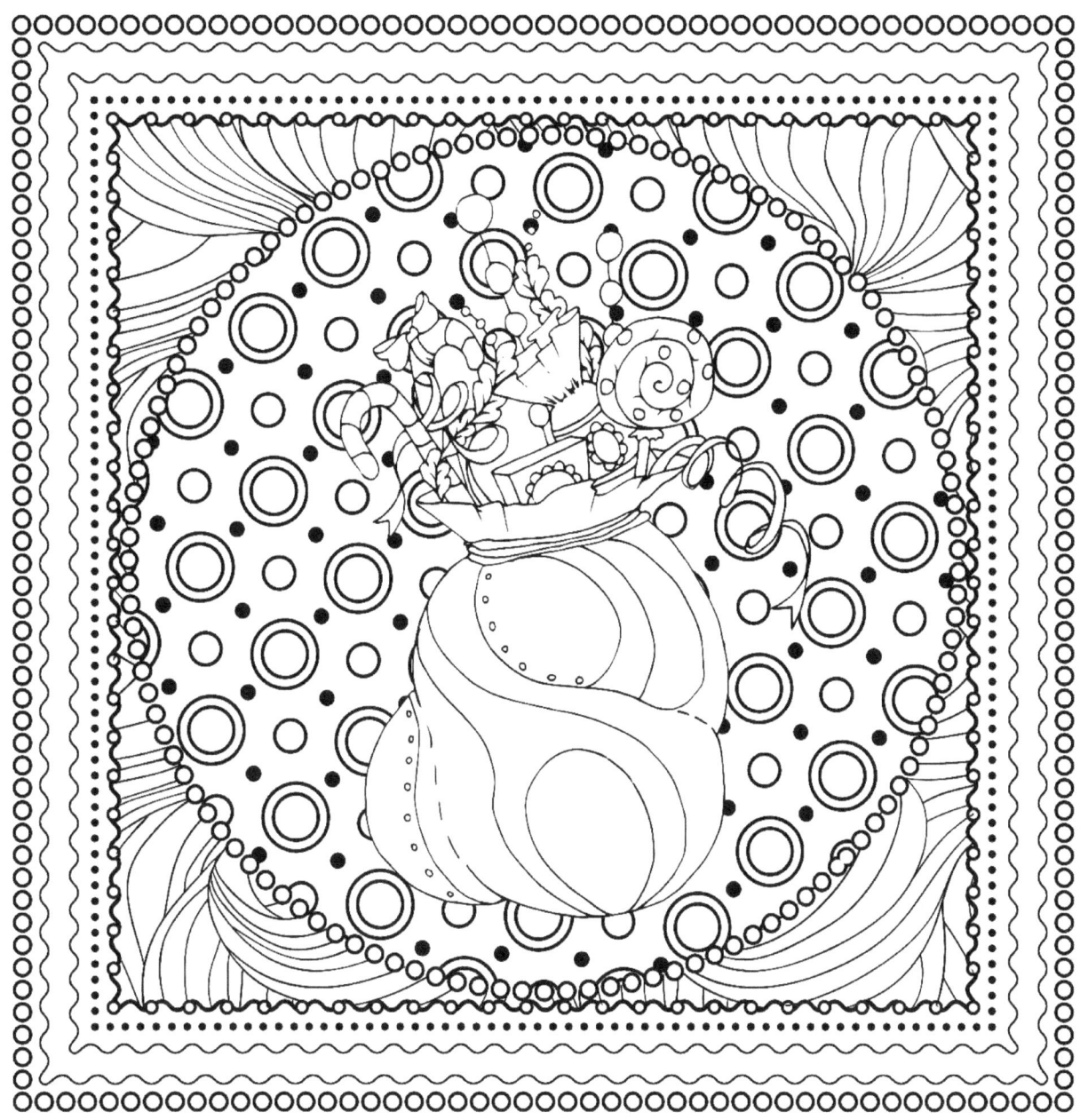

8

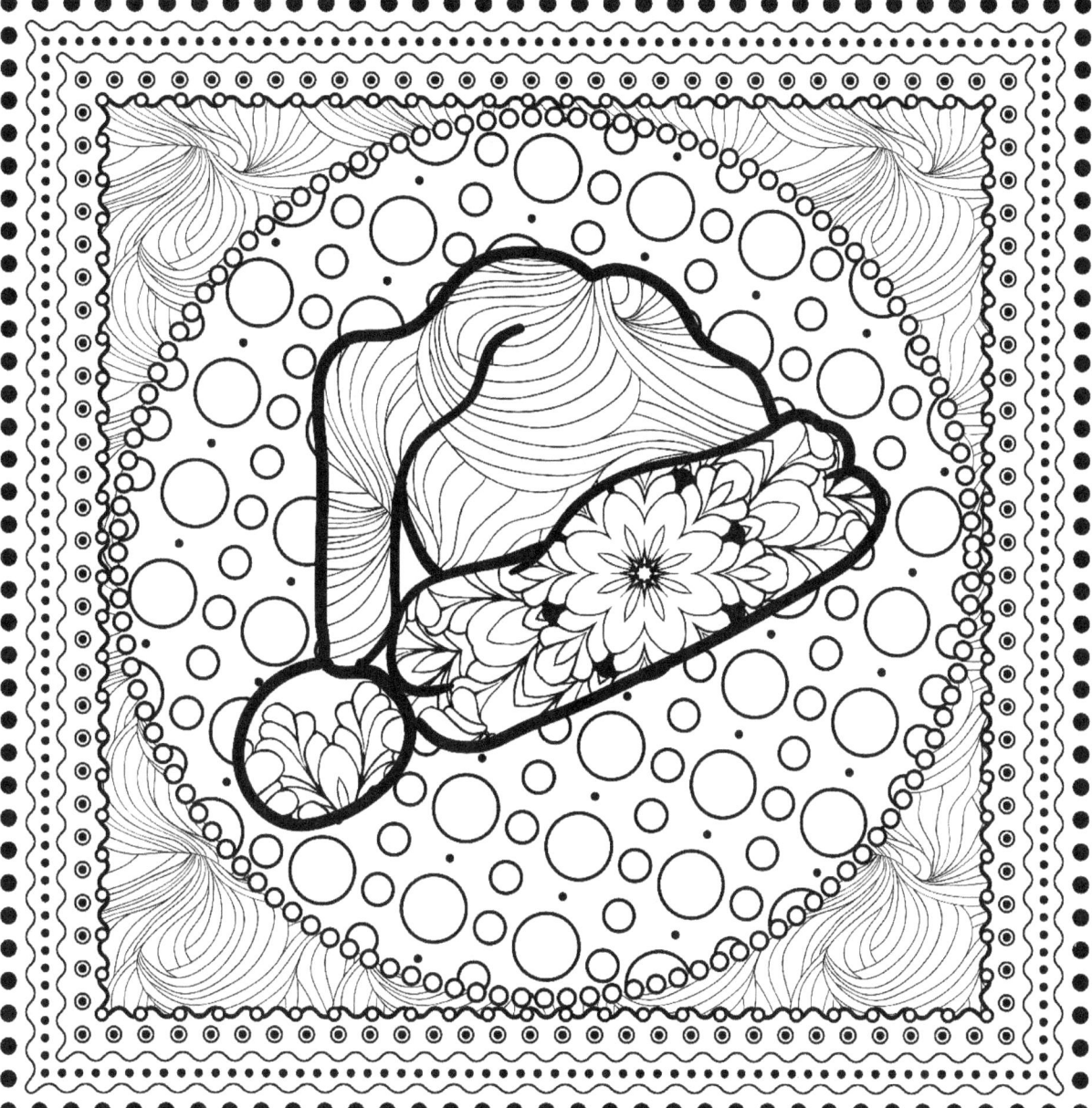

9

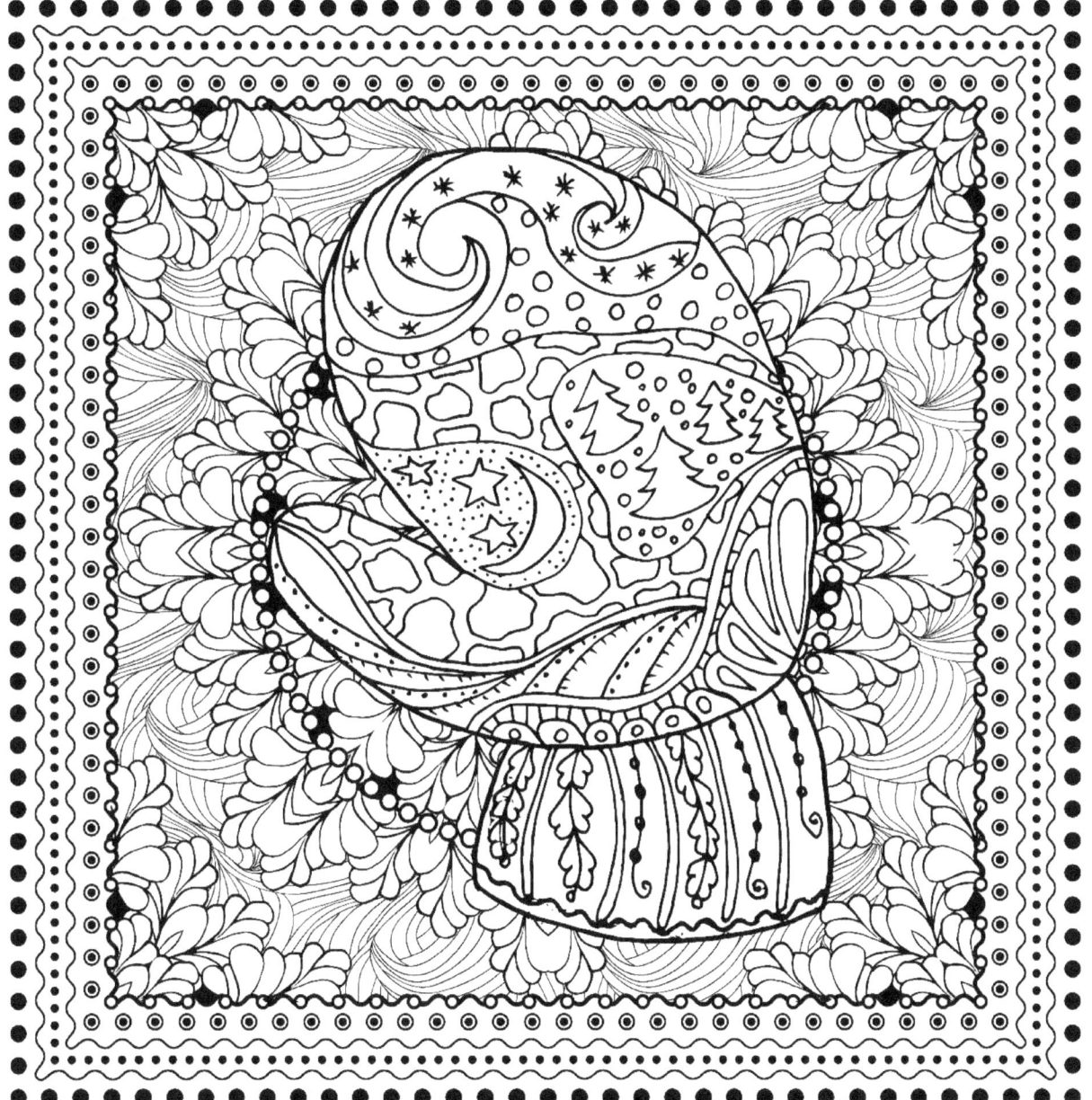

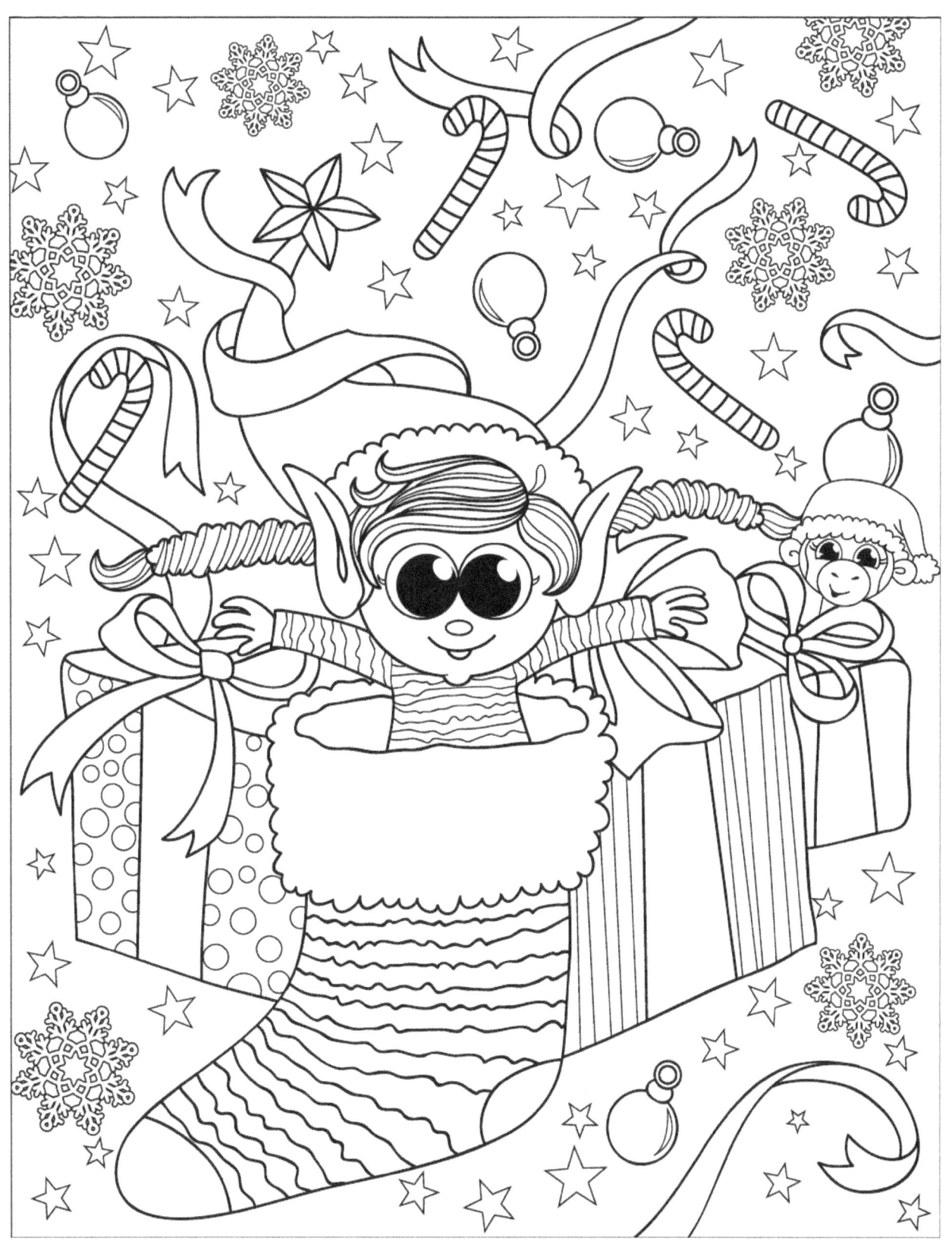

11

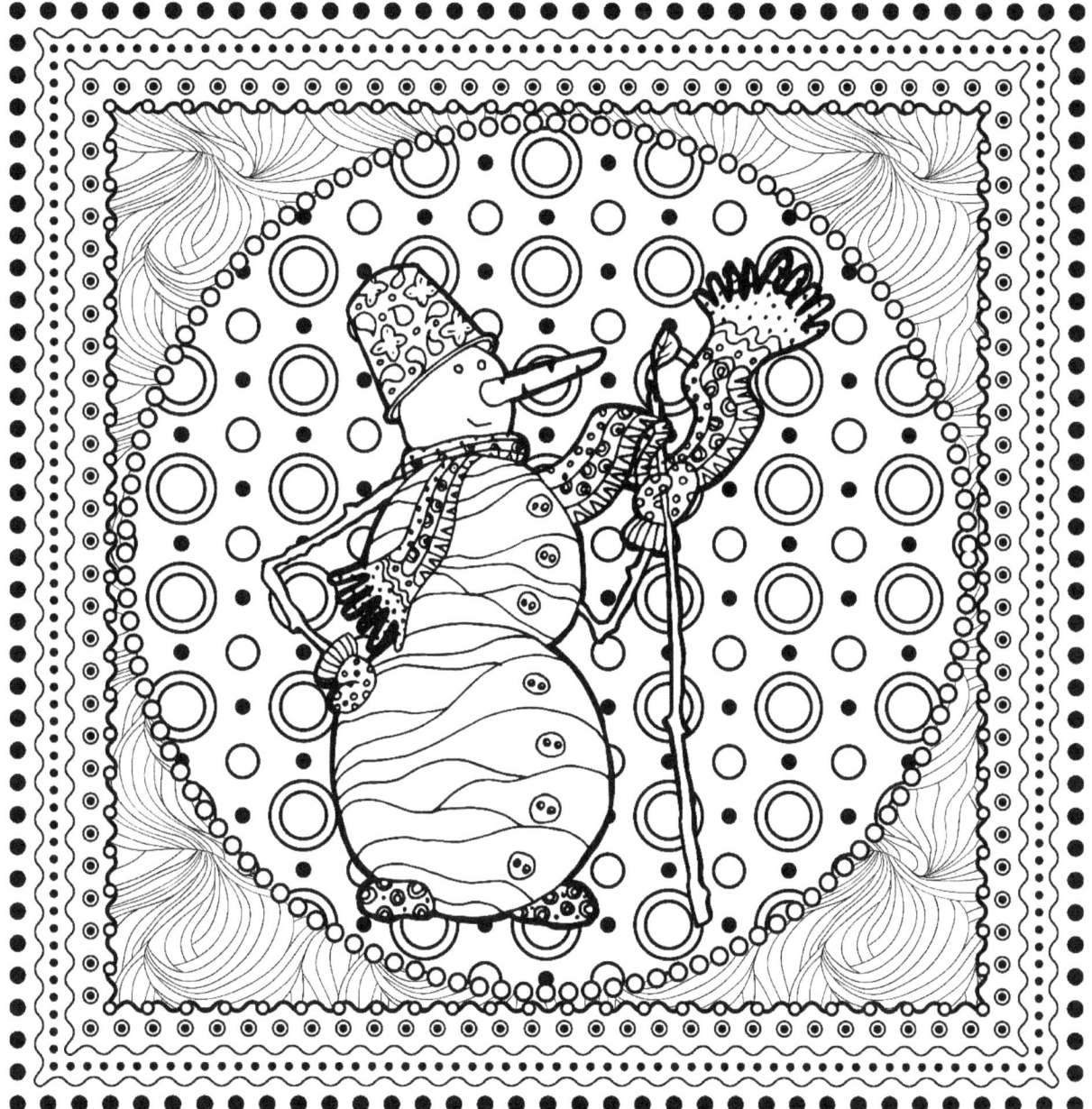

12

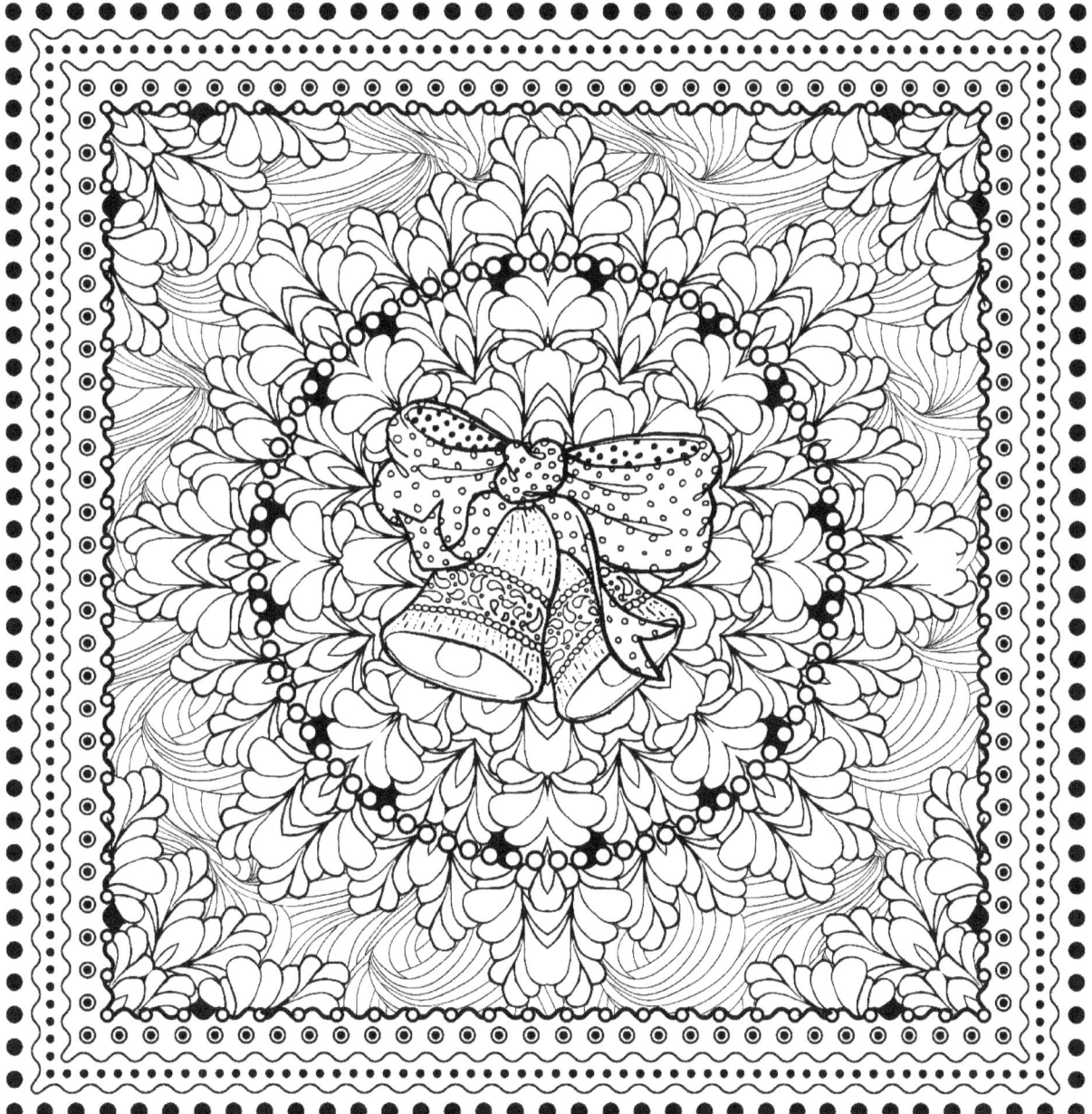

13

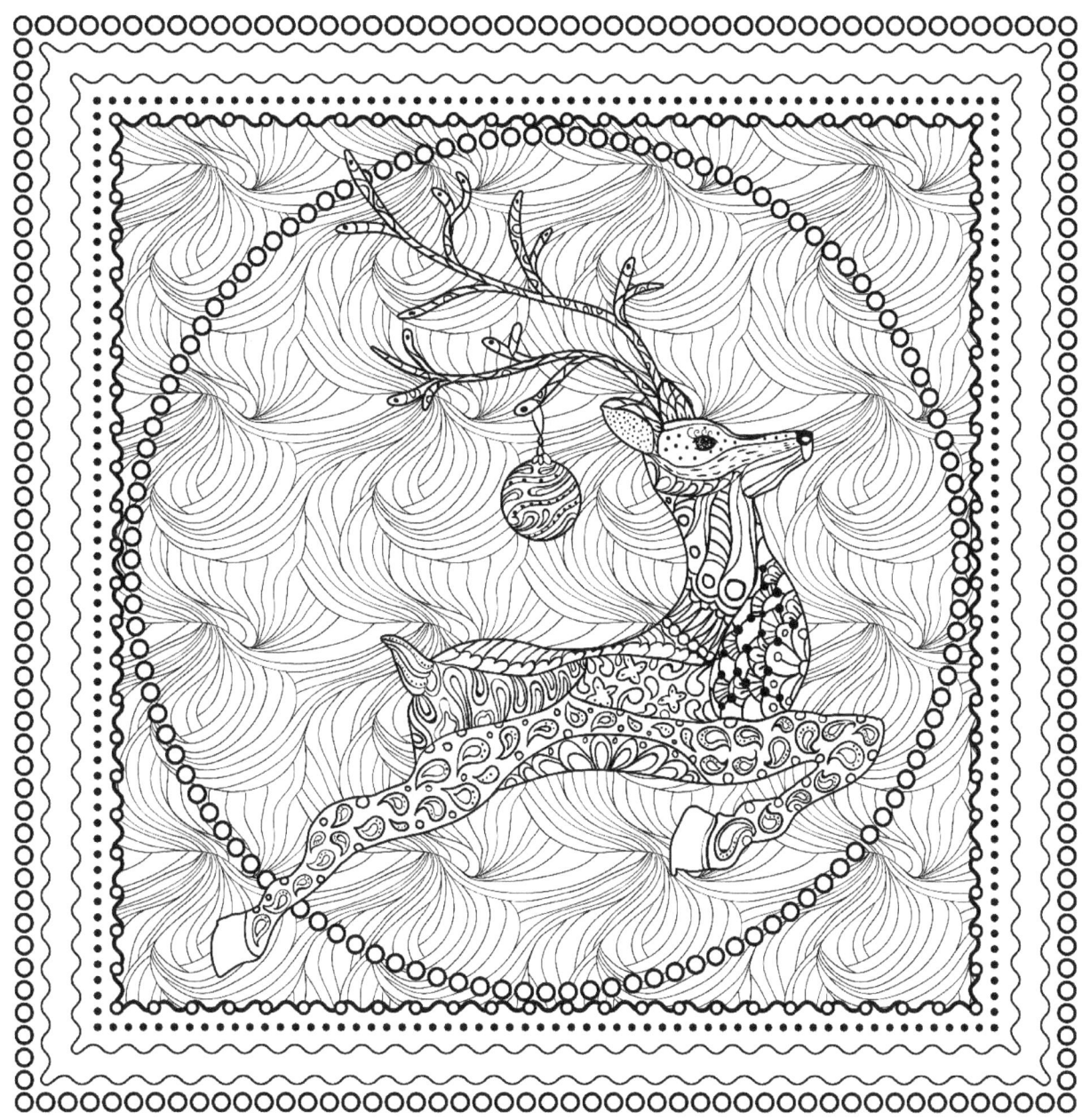

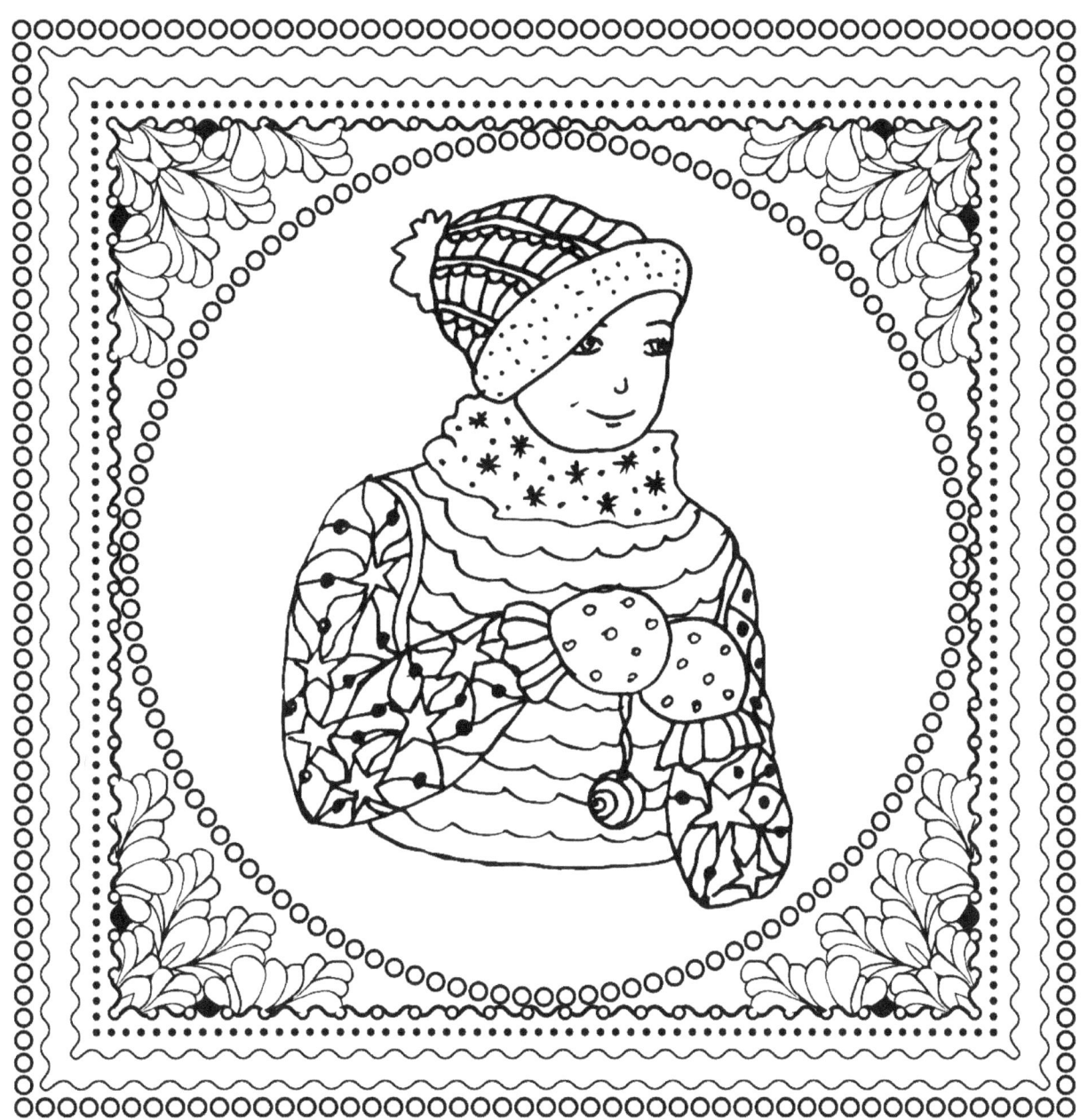

15

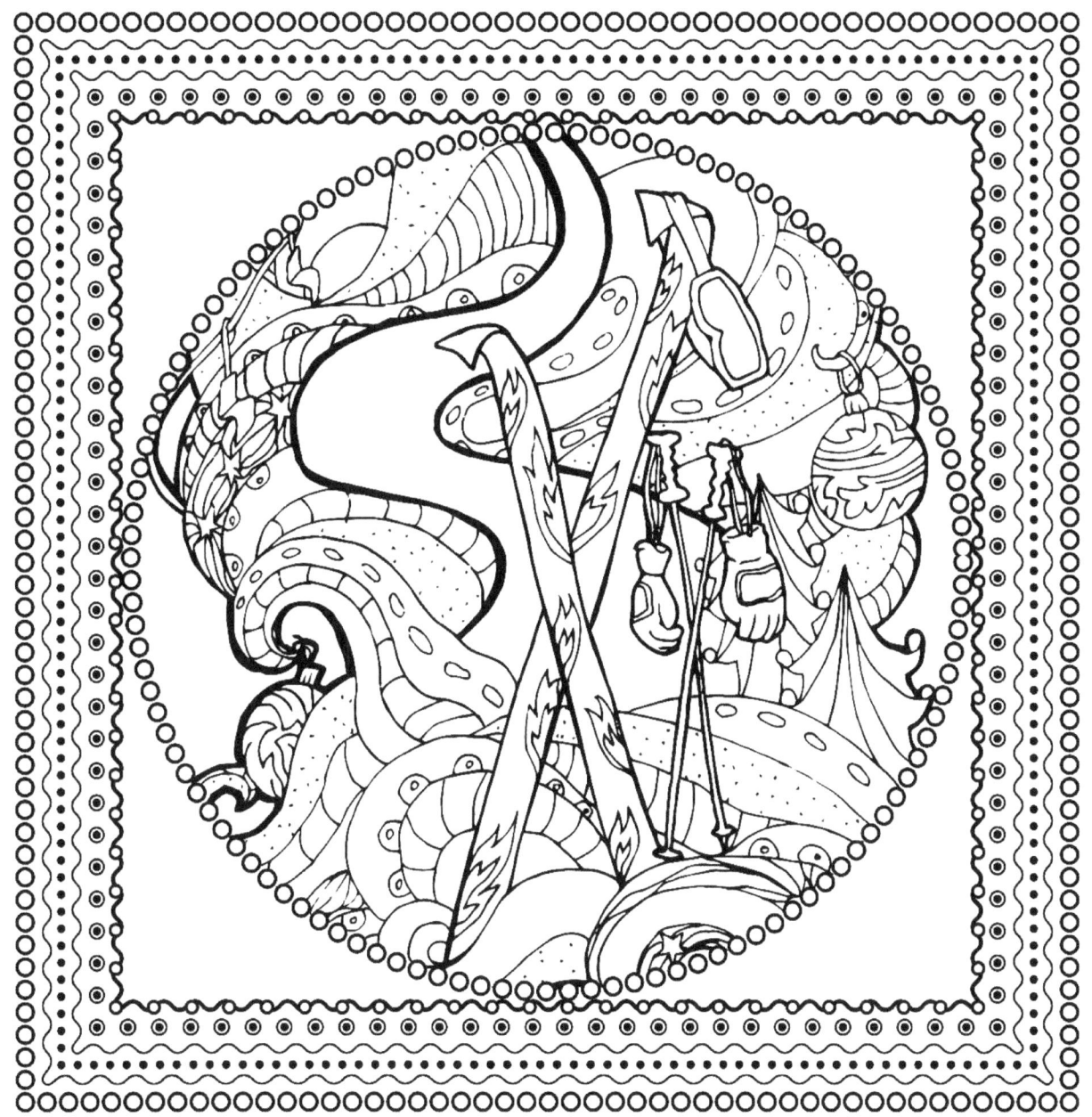

16

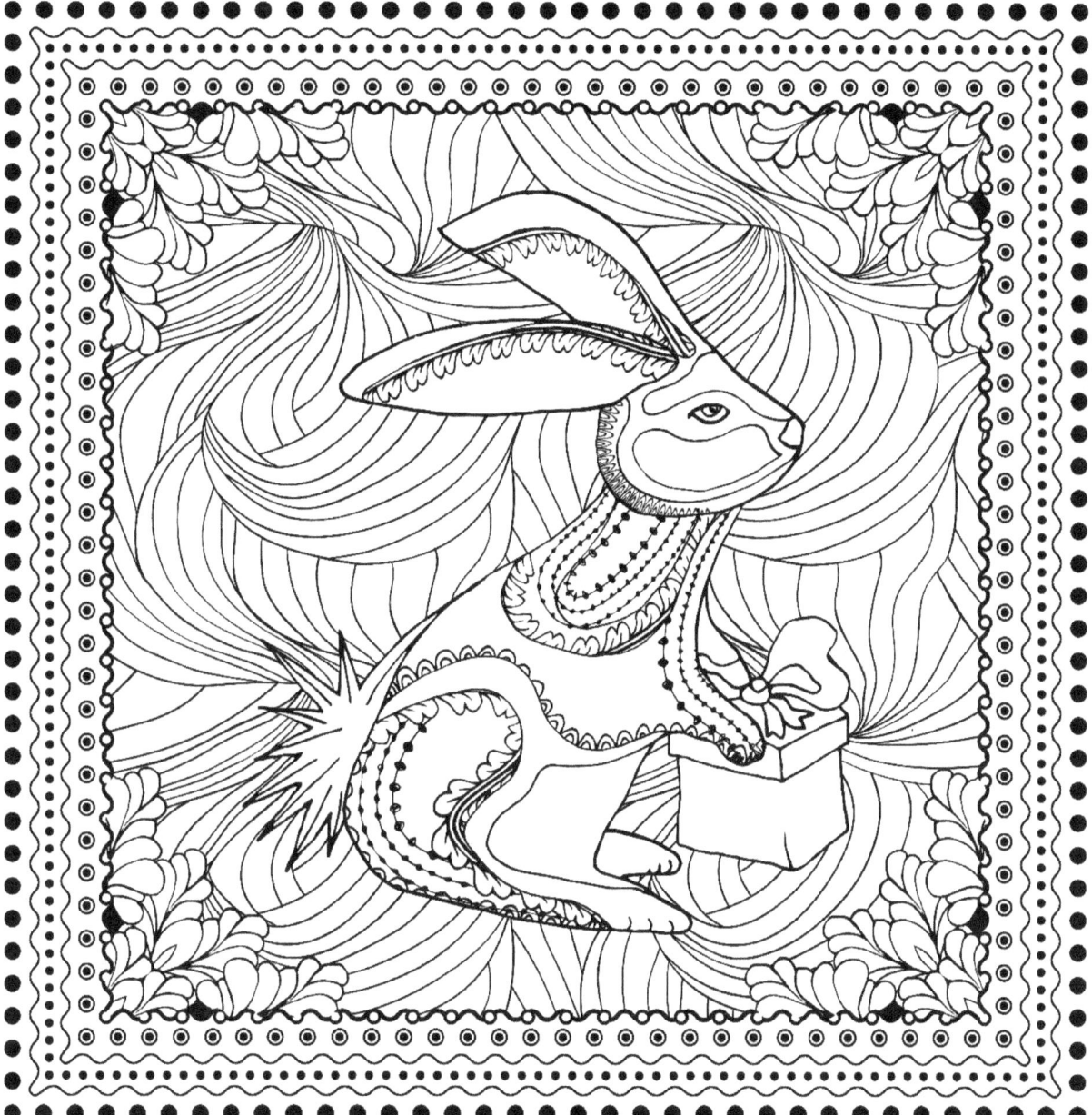

17

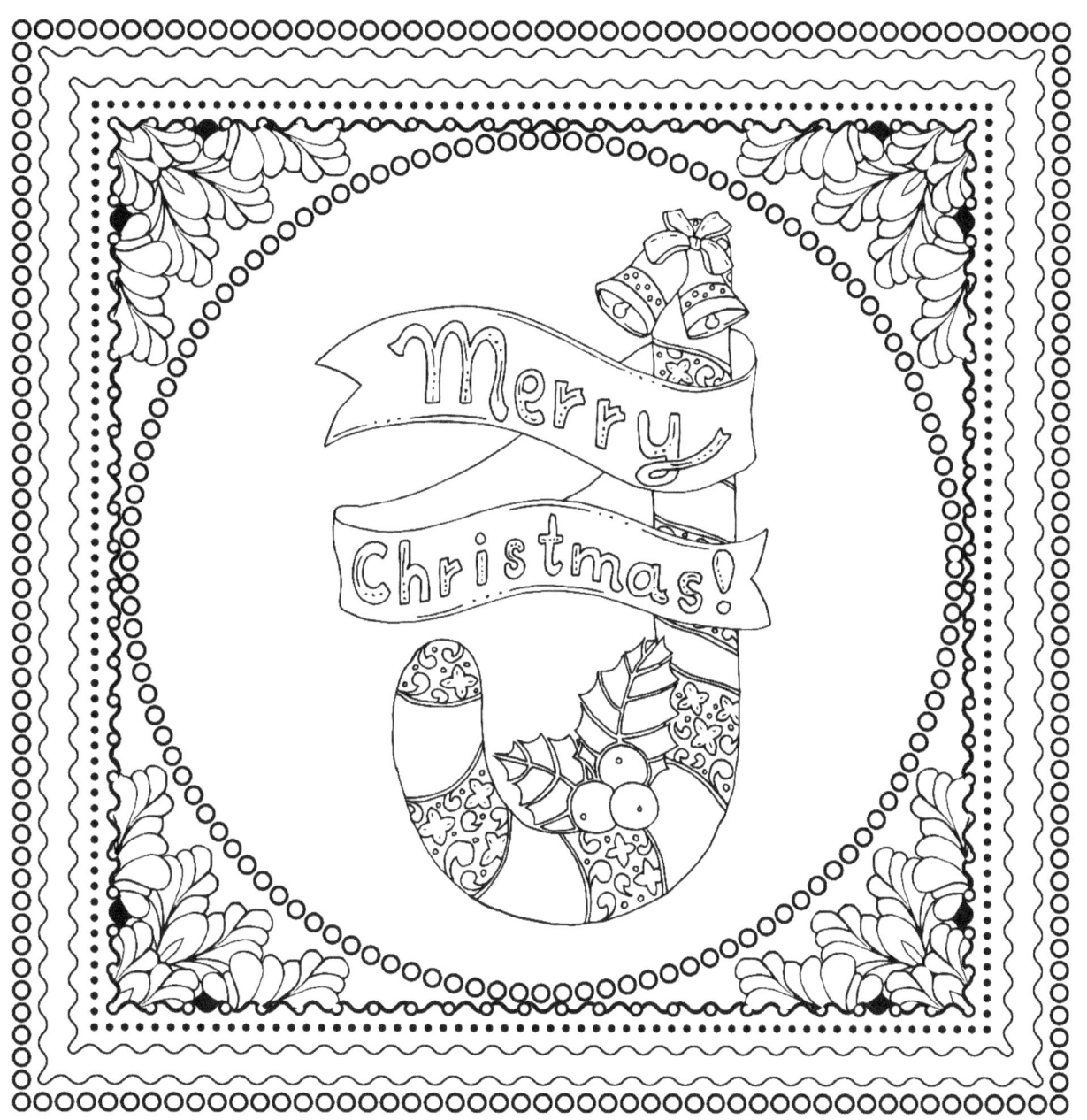

18

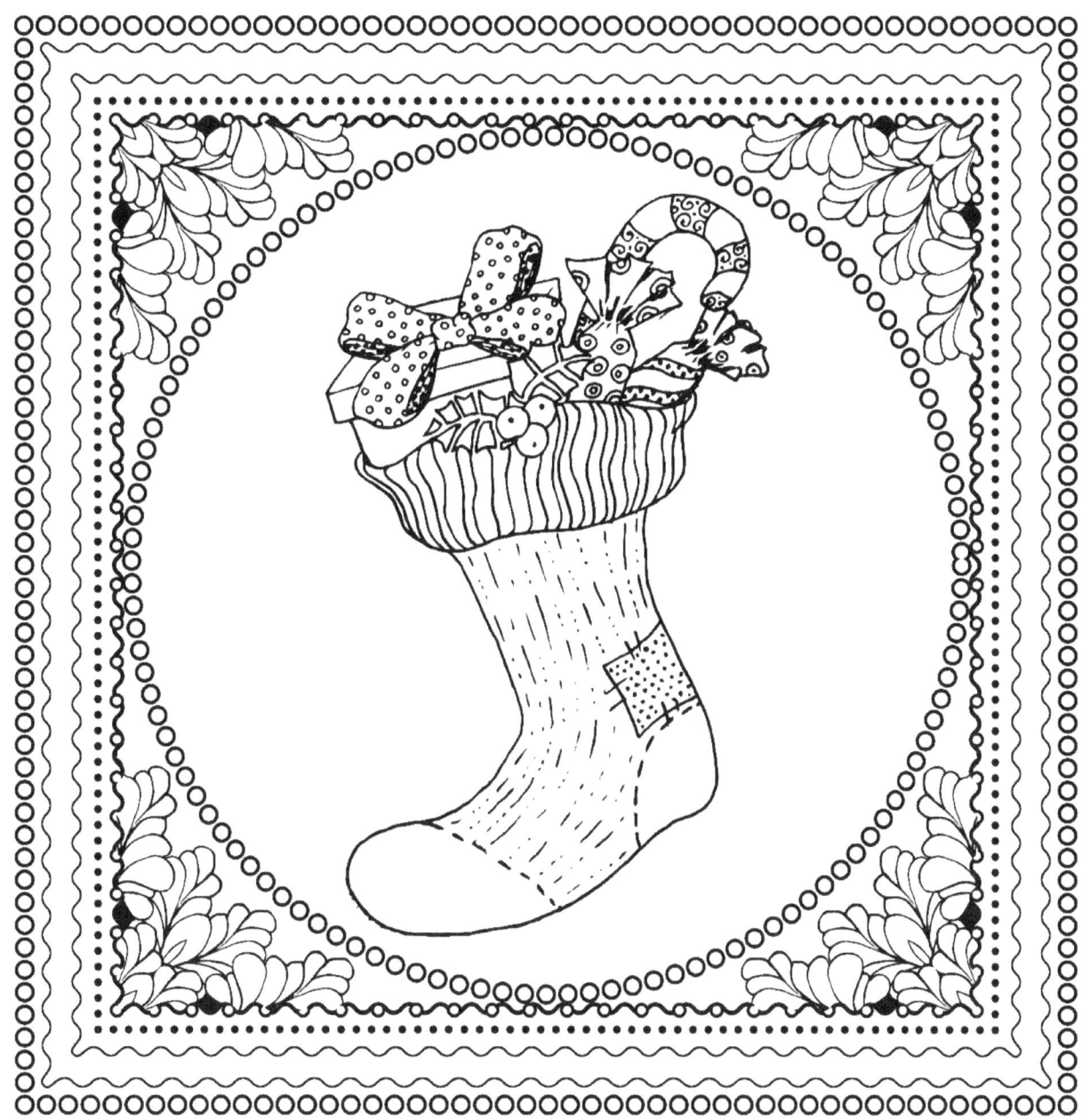

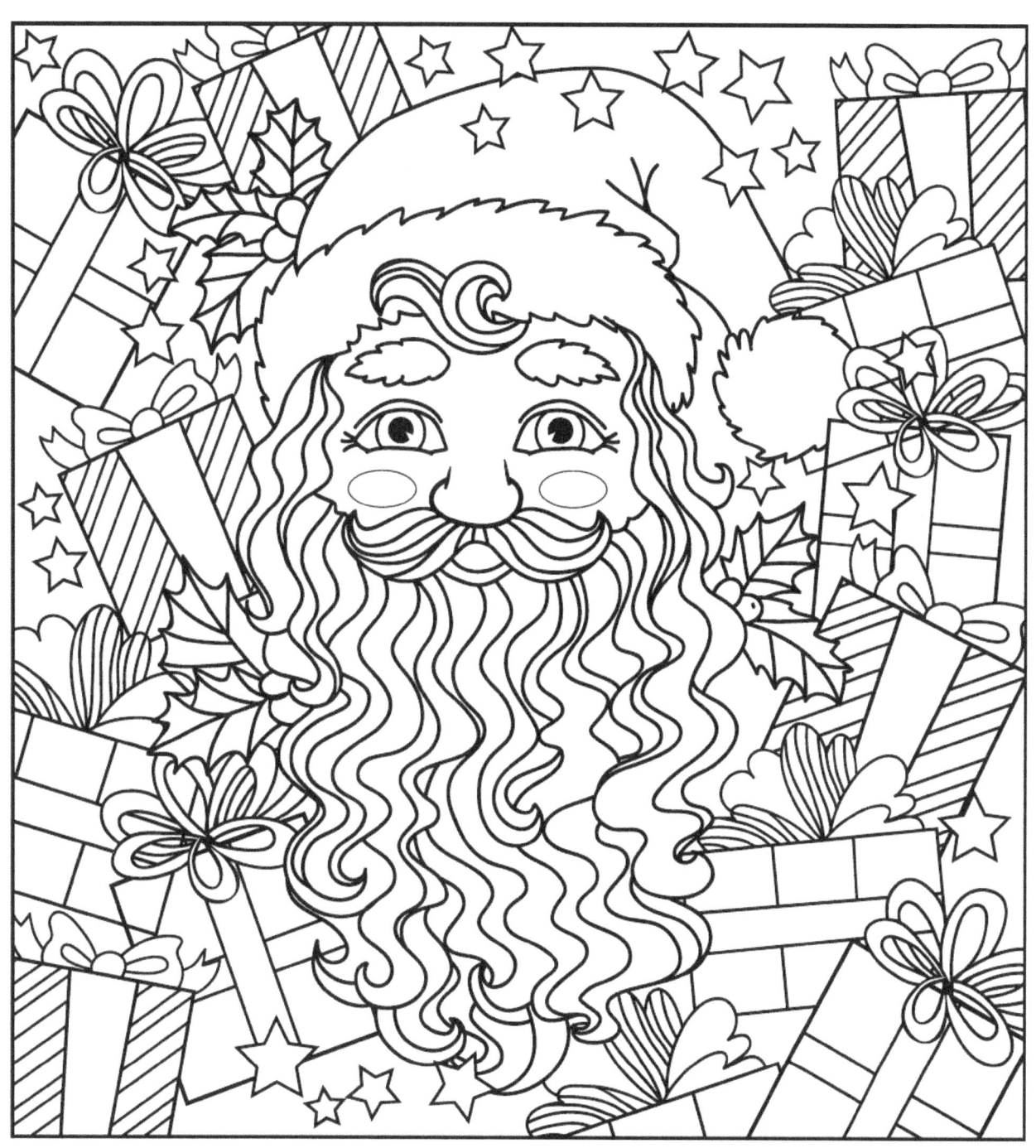

20

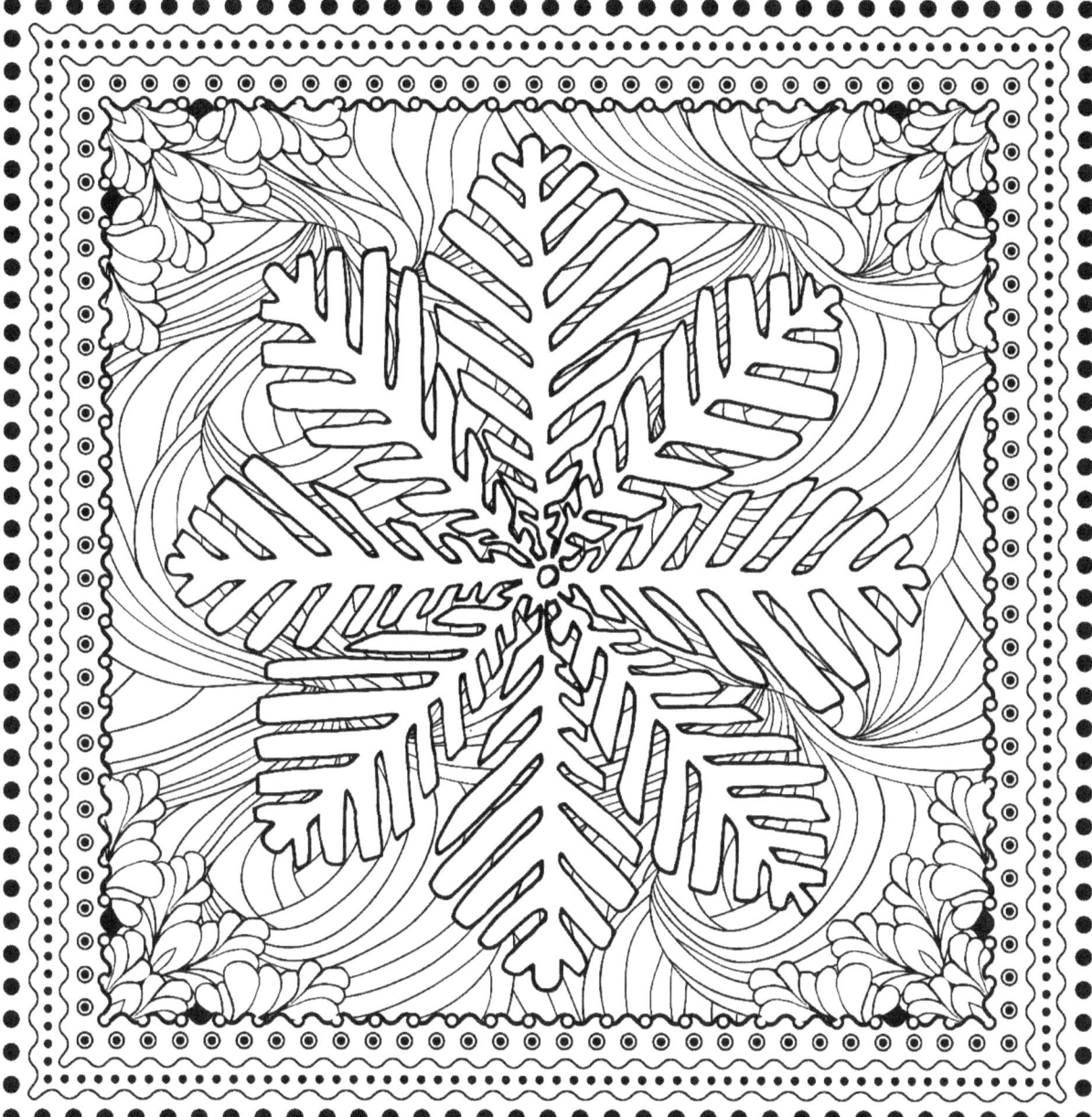

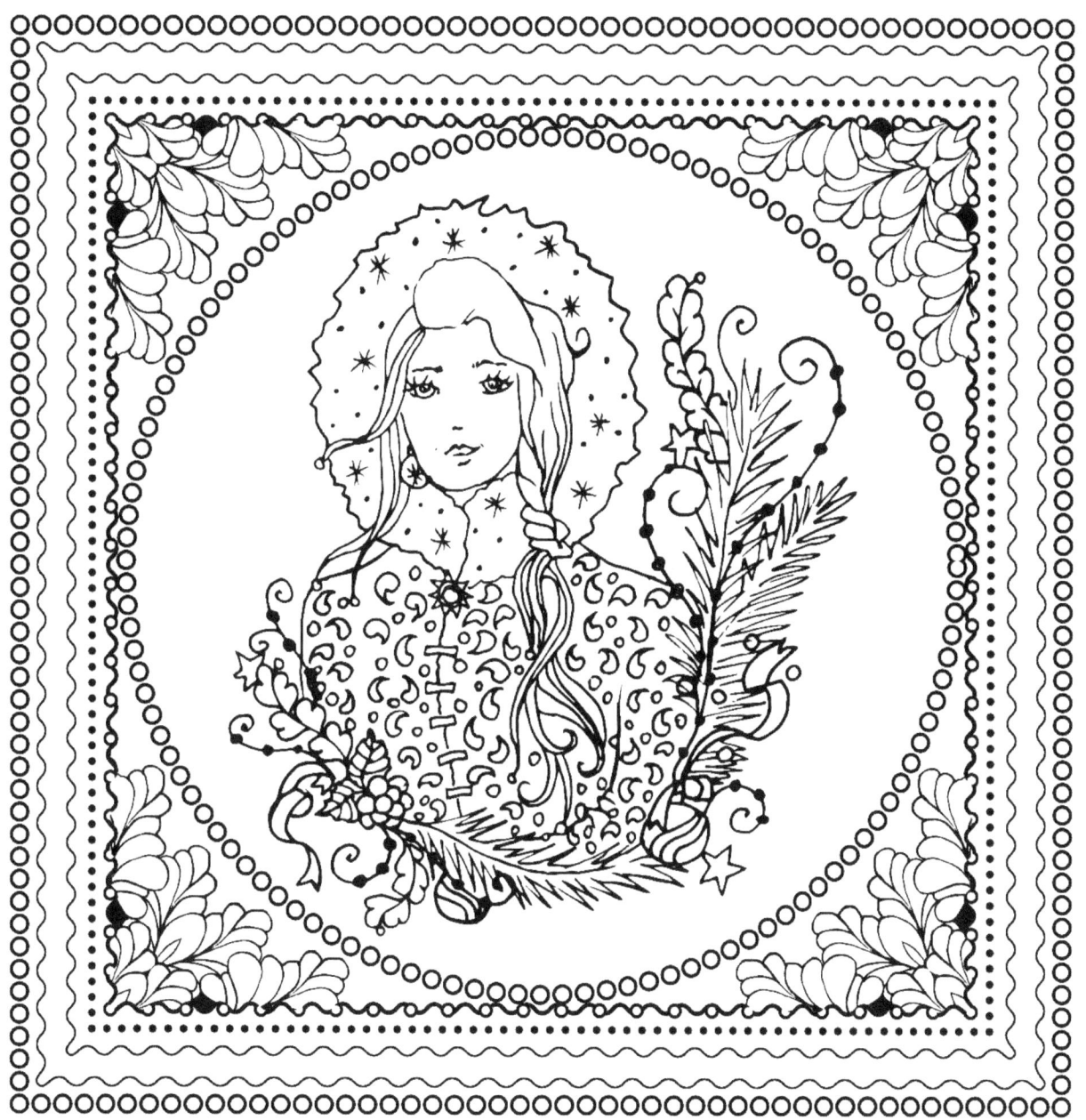

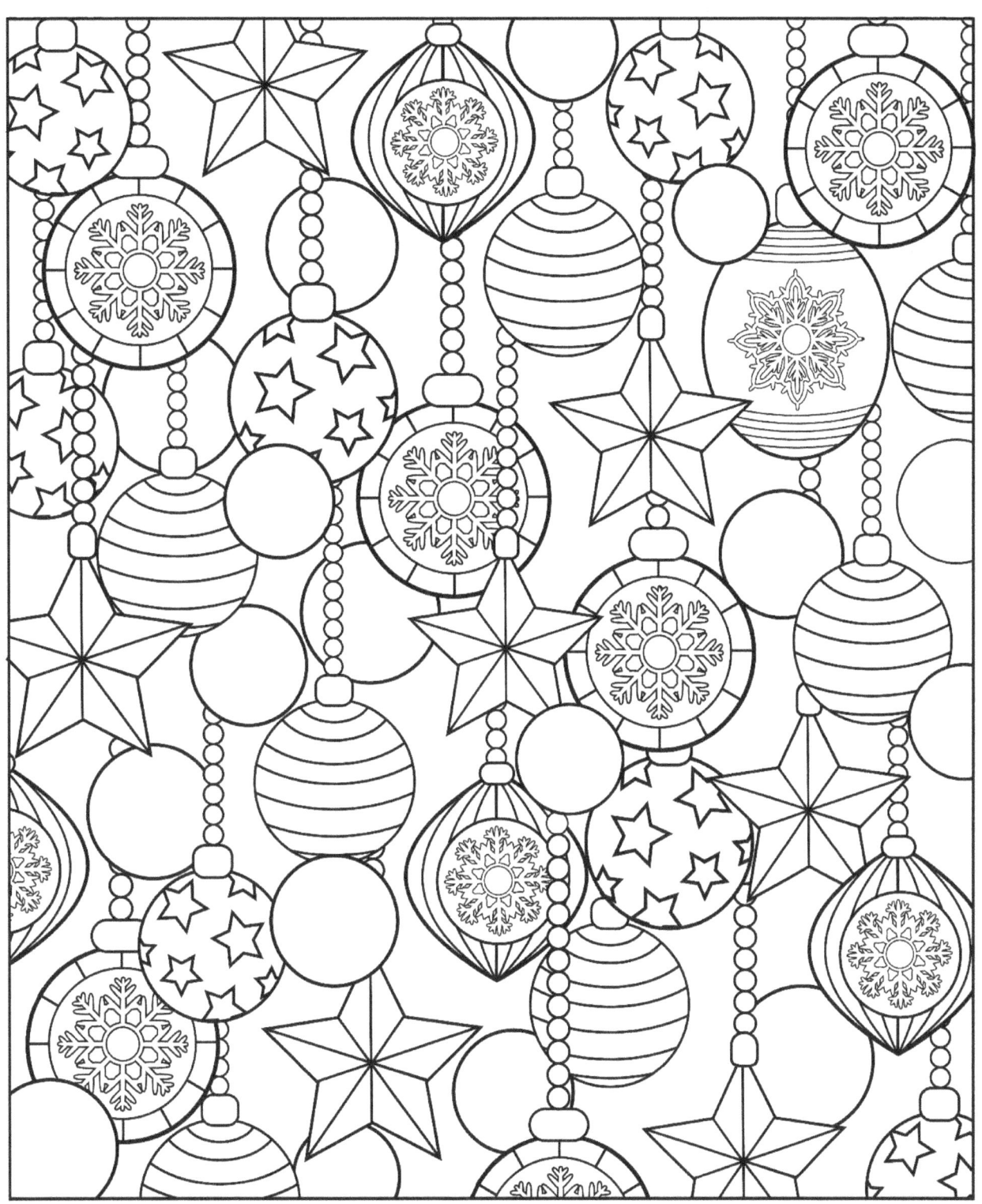

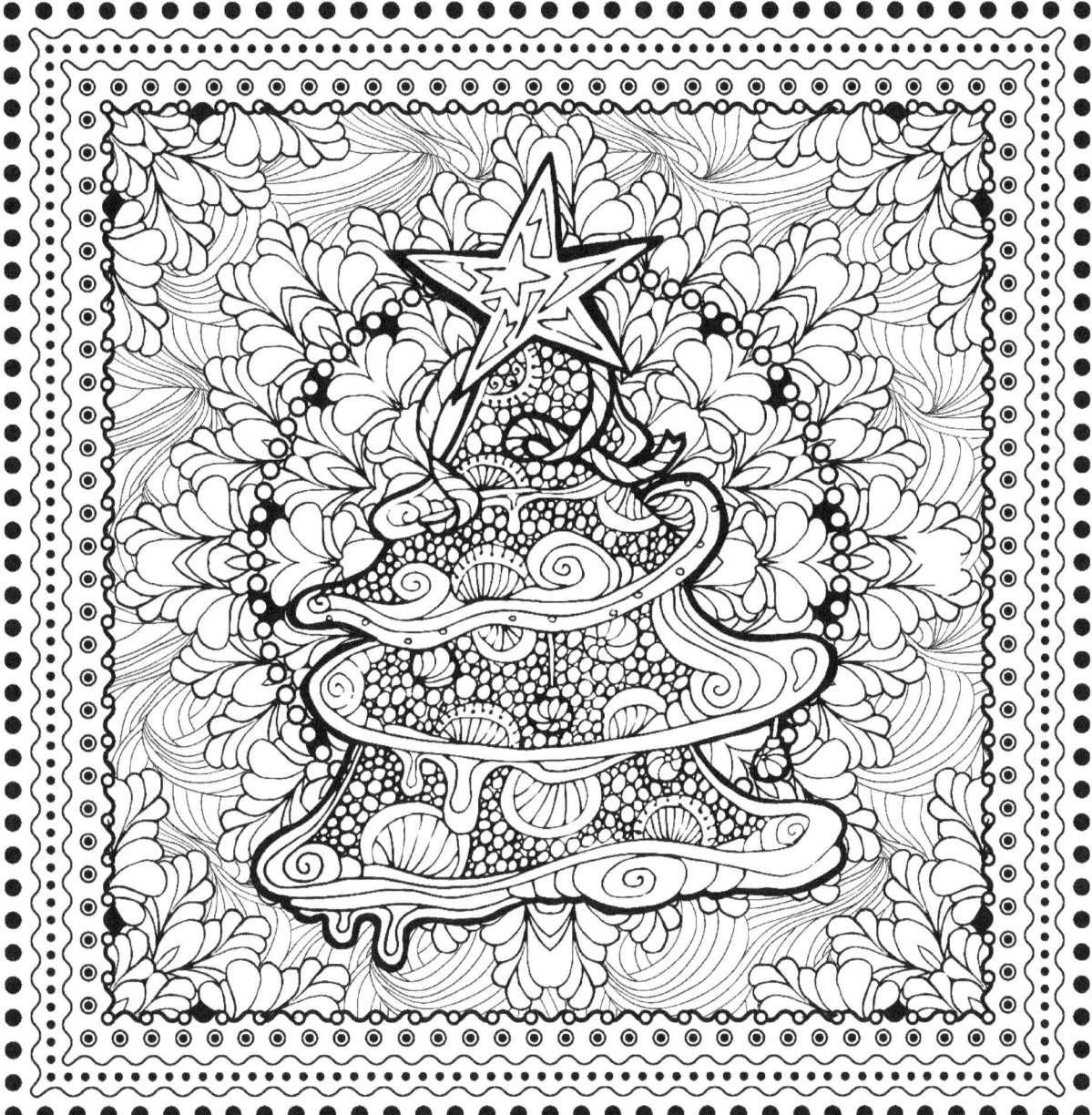

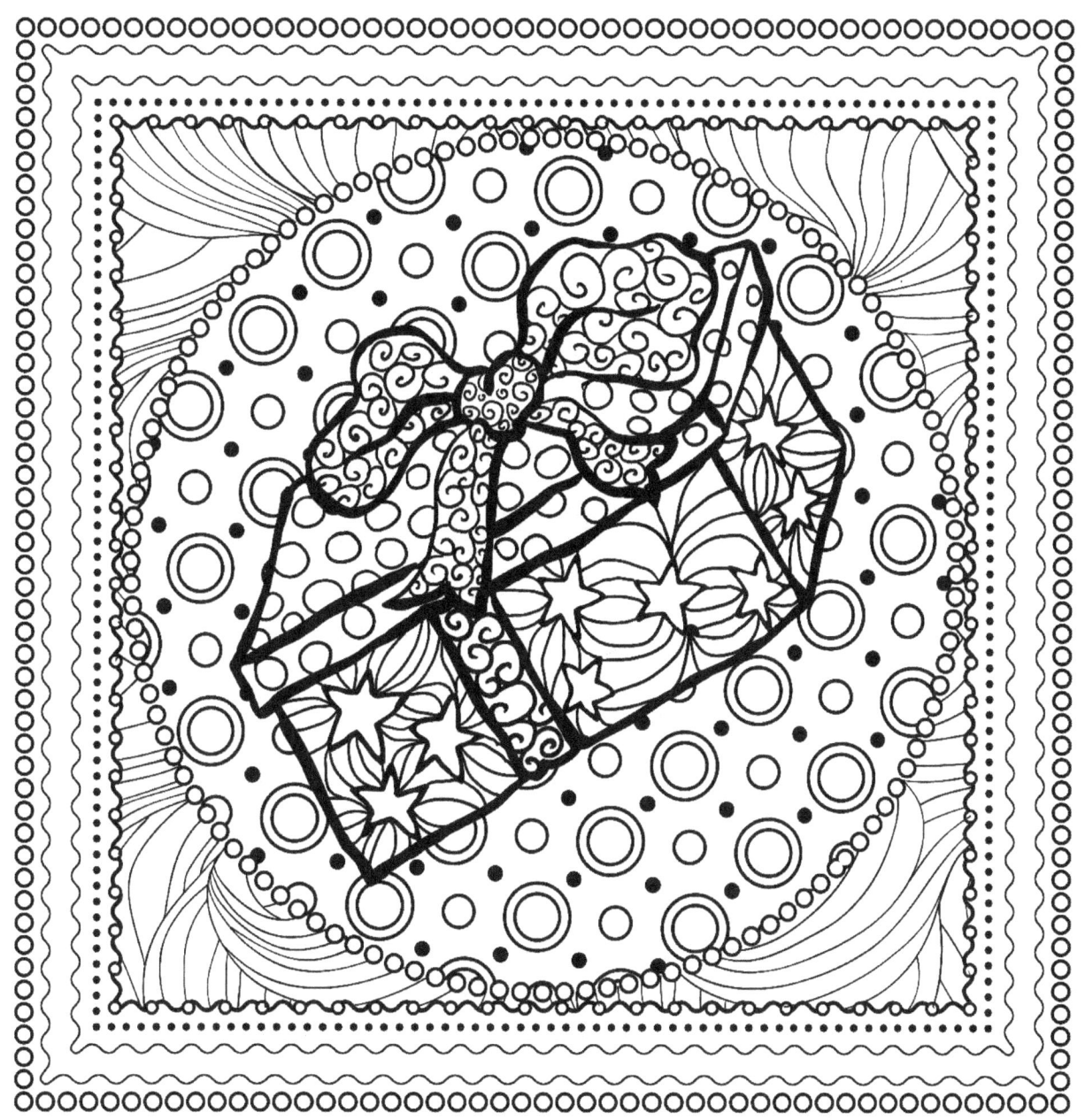

25

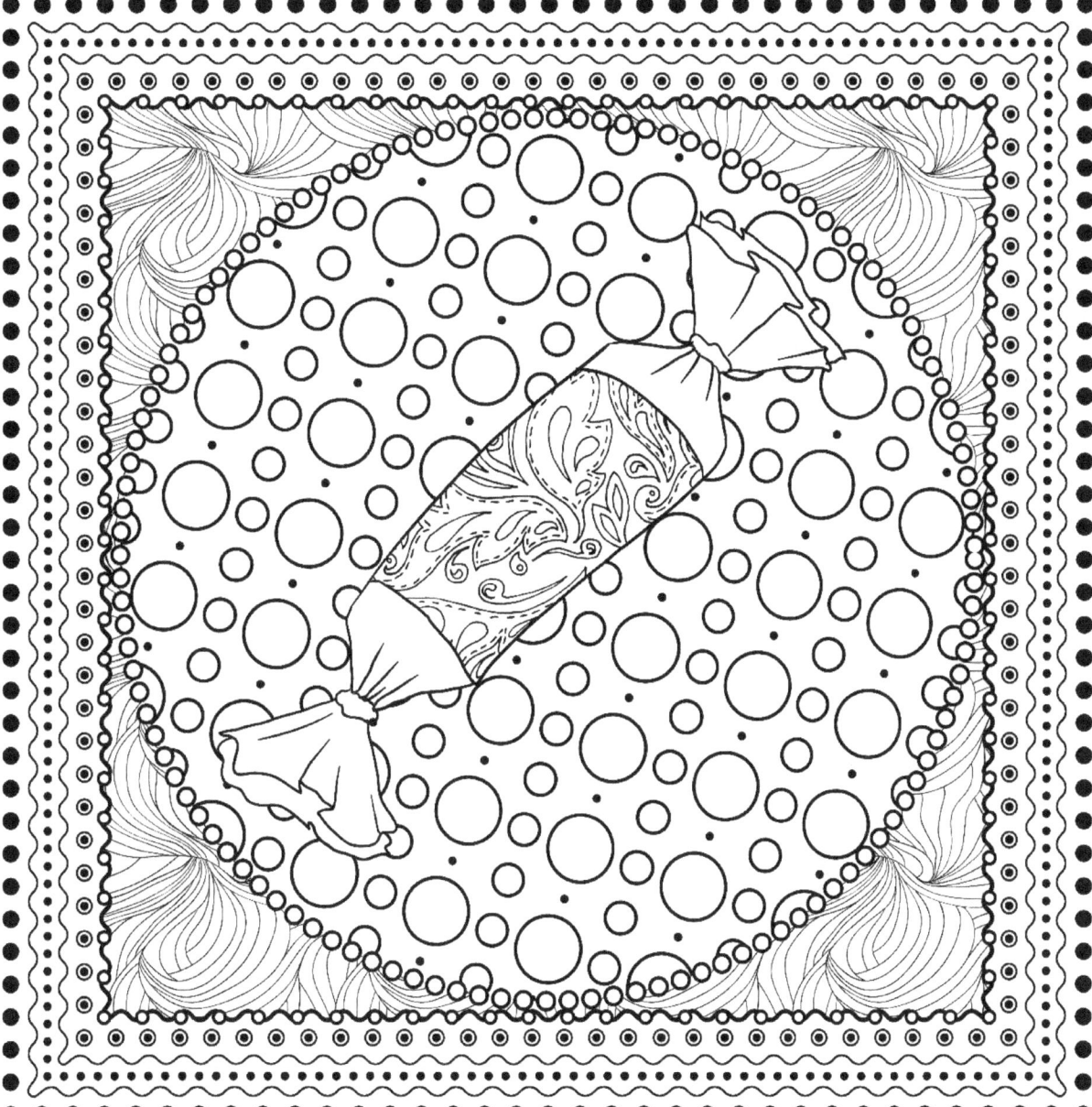

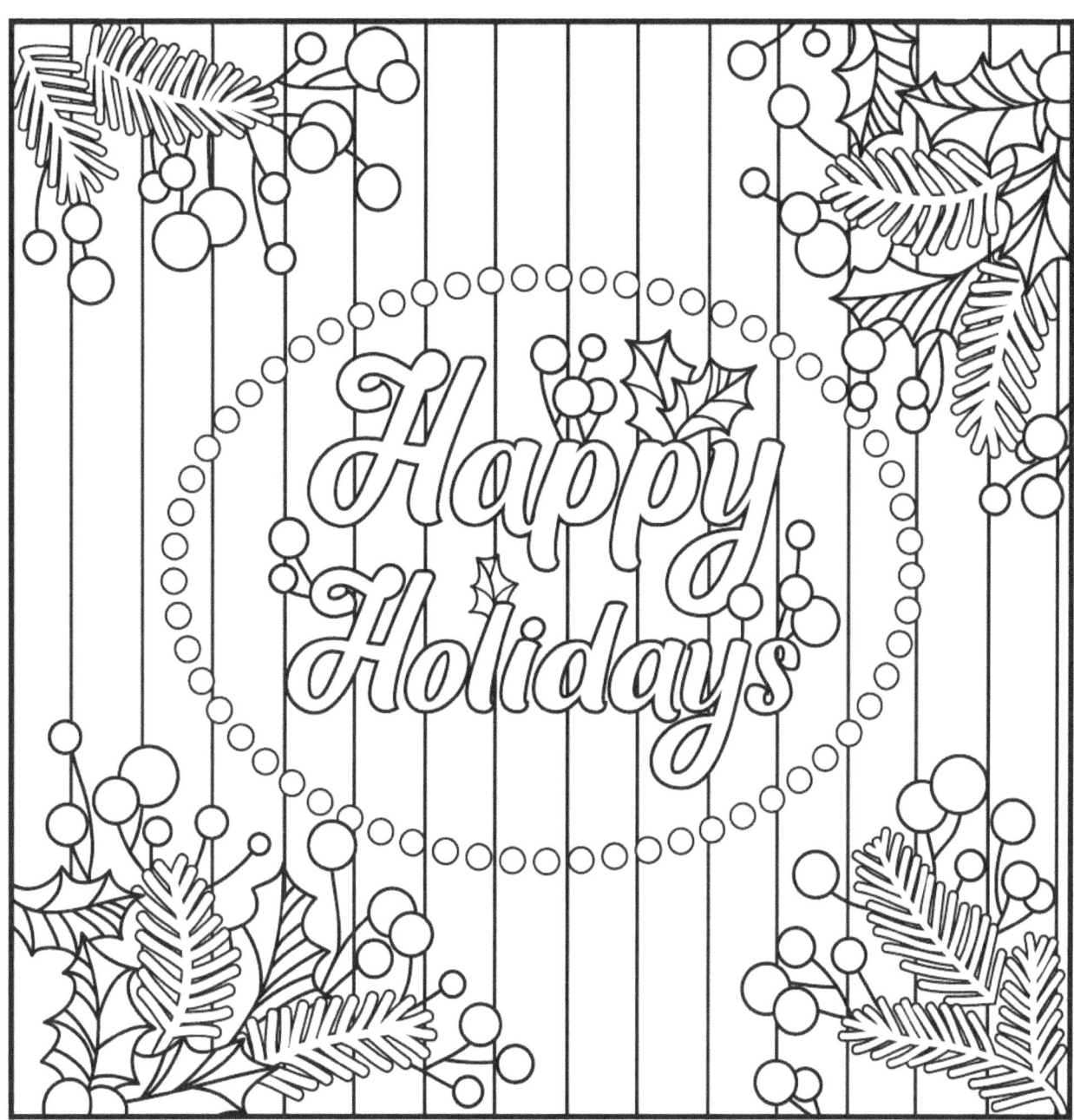

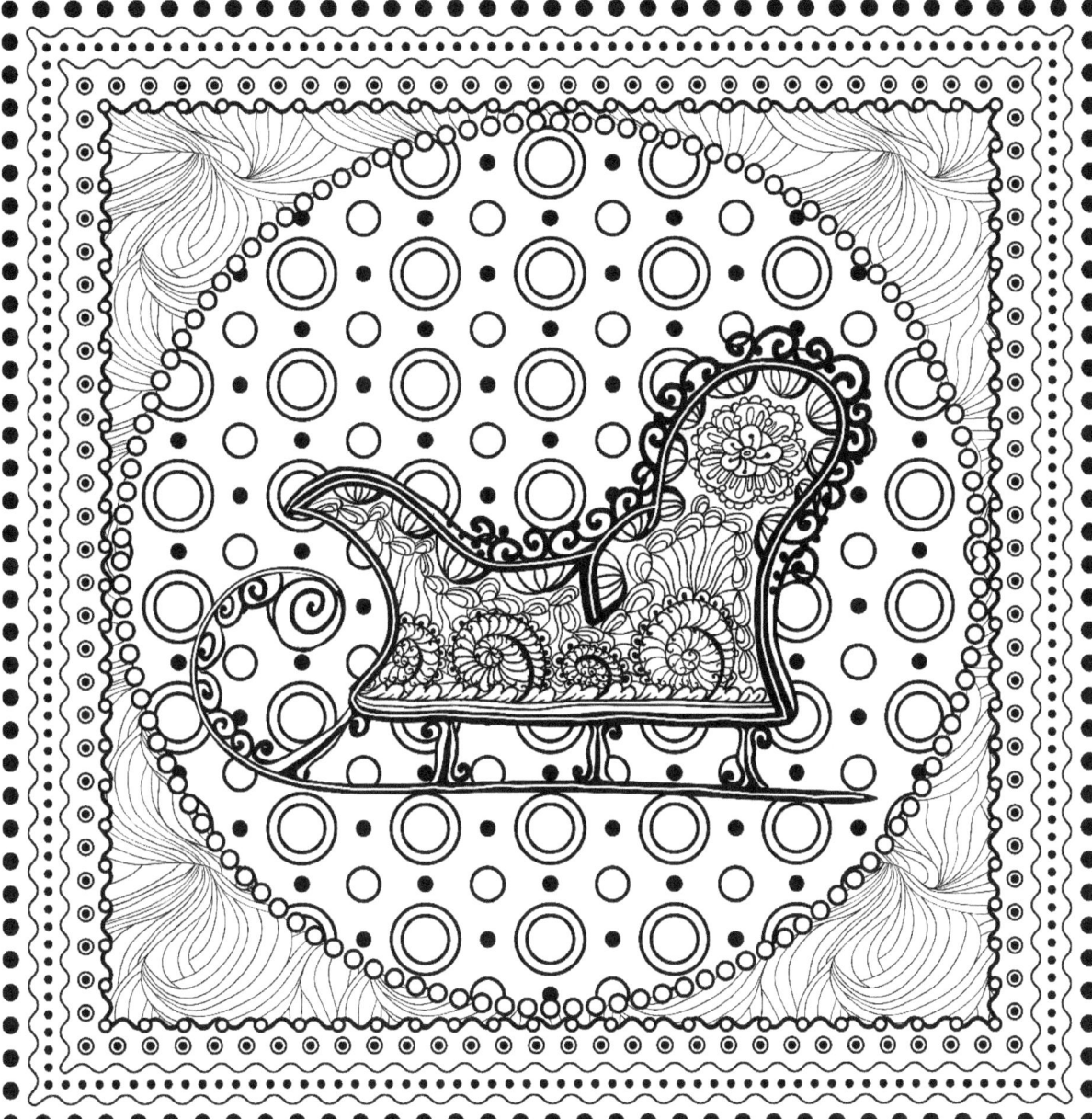

28

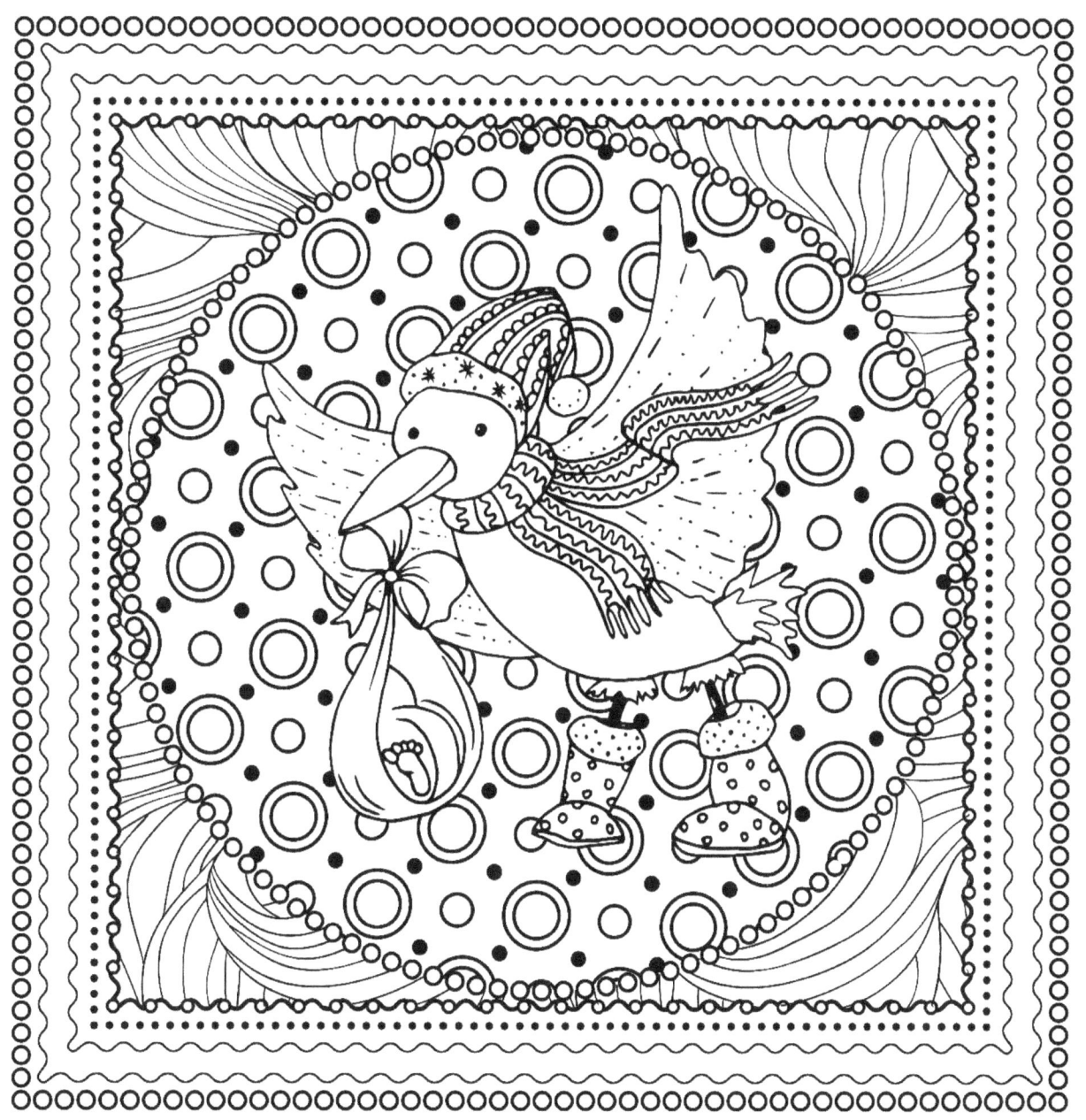

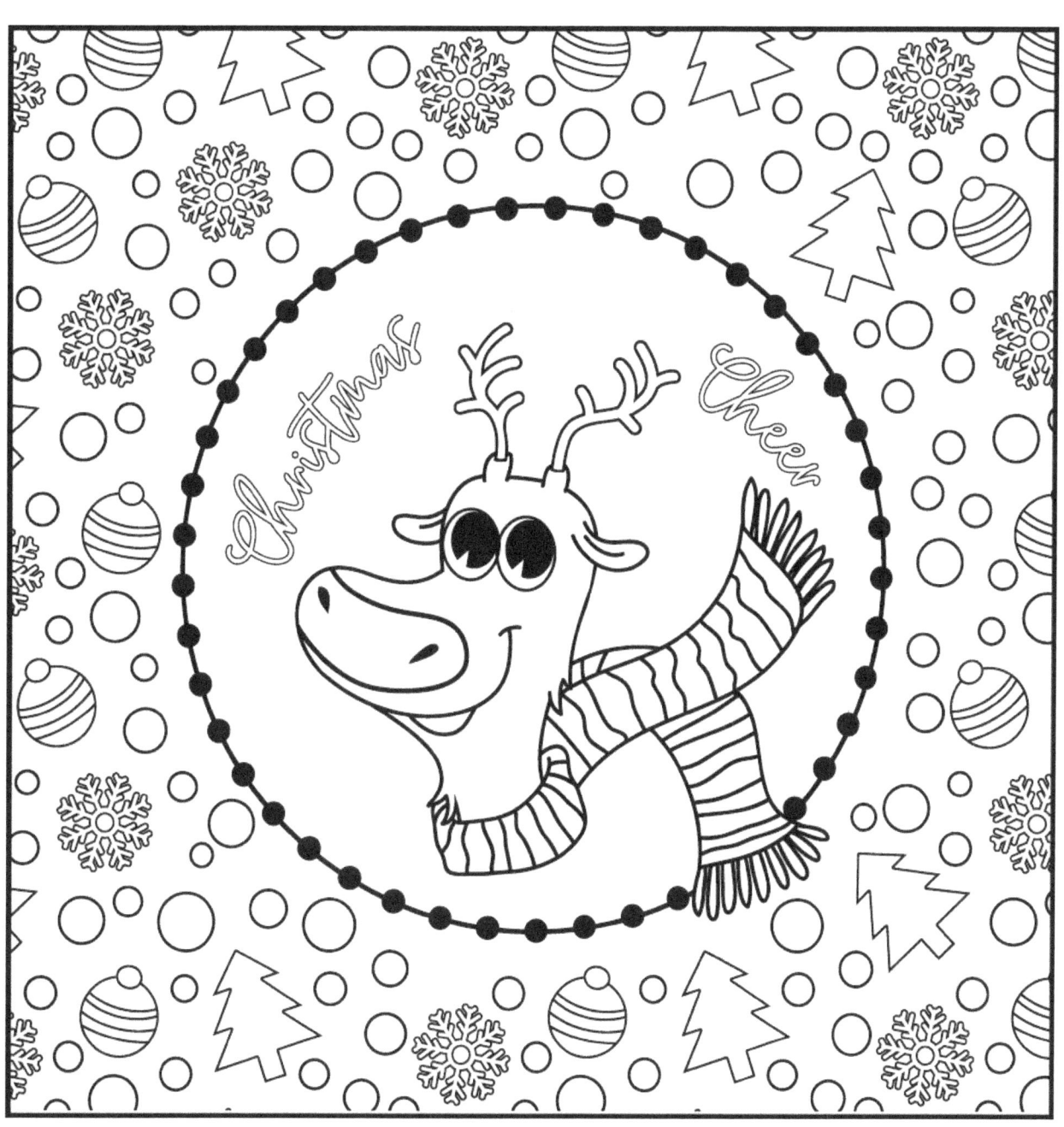

www.ingramcontent.com/pod-product-compliance
Lightning Source LLC
Chambersburg PA
CBHW081500220526
45466CB00008B/2731